Top Twenty Reasons Why:
You aren't getting Job Offers after an Interview

A.J. Diamond

ISBN-10:1518635032
ISBN-13:978-1518635038

Contents

ACKNOWLEDGMENTS

Thank you to all the employers and candidates that allowed me to observe their interviews. In particular, Steve Parr who happily discussed appointment issues for hours on end..

Playing the Interview Game

Applying for jobs? Getting interviews? But then struggling to convert interviews into job offers?

Interviews are still a key part of any job application and offer. However, they are a game – which means that anyone can learn how to do well in an interview. Key is to ensure you play the correct game.

Consider Roger Federer or Serena Williams turning up for the final at Wimbledon or Flushing Meadows. Out of their bag they take a hockey stick. Do you really think they will win their game of tennis playing with a hockey stick?

I'm keeping my money in my pocket. Trying to win a game of tennis playing with a hockey stick is just 'not playing the game'!

It is exactly the same with job interviews. You need to know the rules and play with the right equipment if you want to have a chance.

This book gives you the top twenty reasons why people fail or do poorly in job interviews. To do well in your job interviews, learn the rules – then play the game.

Start with reason number 1 – it is the most common reason why people do poorly or less well than they are capable of in job interviews. Make sure you understand and address this reason above all others.

When you are satisfied that you know how to make sure that you will not make that mistake, work through the remaining 19 reasons – checking them off as you develop a plan for ensuring YOU don't make those mistakes.

I would wish you good luck with your job interview – but if you have worked through these Top Twenty Reasons, you won't need luck. You will be in a great position to do well in your job interview.

Getting to the Interview

Pre-Interview Check #1

Before looking at the Top Twenty Reasons Why anyone is likely to do poorly at interview, it is important to recognize that you have actually got to be invited to an interview.

This implies that you are "in the ball park" of being suitable for the role.

For example, if you are a plumber and are applying to become the chief electrician, it is unlikely that you will get an interview. That is, you are playing a different game from that of "electrician".

Another example could be that you are a marketing manager and apply for the post of surgeon at the local hospital.

The point here is that it can be very difficult to gain interviews for roles where you are clearly unqualified for that position.

This doesn't mean that you can't become an electrician or surgeon – but before you gain paid (or even unpaid) employment in such a role, you must acquire some of the knowledge and skills required for that particular field of work.

Pre-Interview Check #2

For most positions you will need to provide several references. A show stopper is a bad reference from one of your referees.

In the UK, you are entitled to see what any organization writes about you – so if you are either not making it to any interview or you are gaining interviews which go well, but then fall over at the reference part, you need to check out what people are saying about you.

While many organizations will simply provide the basic reference of "worked here between dates X and Y", some organizations can hold grudges against employees. Actually it is usually a boss who has placed a negative reference in your file – and the admin people simply provide it.

If this is the case – you need to challenge that reference. Get some legal advice (Go to the Citizens Advice Bureau in the first place if you are in the UK). Alternatively, pay for some employment law advice from a lawyer/solicitor – use a specialist one (not one who does house conveyancing!)

Make sure you build a range of references from different types of people. For example, if you do any sort of course for anything – where the tutor or teacher gets to know you over a period of time (anything over 4 months is good), ask them if they will act as a referee for you. The worst that they can say is "No" – but few do.

Pre-Interview Check #3

Social Media posts.

It is amazing how many people bad mouth their employer on social media. Then they are surprised when that employer sacks them!

Duh!

This happened to Zoe who posted some indiscrete posts while under the influence of drink. Two days later, she was without a job. Gaining a new job took her over a year! The job she got was at a significantly lower level than her previous job and she had undertaken a lot of voluntary work to help build an alternative reference.

However, Zoe still had to explain why she had left that original job at interview. Time having passed, enabled her to reflect on immaturity of youth and the danger of alcohol excess.

Zoe's message – take great care not to gossip or moan on any social media – it will live with you for the rest of your life!

Therefore, this book is based on the interview stage of being selected and offered a job. The screening done before interview normally will check that you are capable of undertaking much of the role requirements – especially any skills which require qualifications.

Reason #1

Know nothing about your prospective employer.

This is usually considered unforgivable. This is the information age – you can find out a host of things about any company or organization through an online search.

Don't have a computer? Go to your local library – they have free use of computers and internet. They also can hold information about big businesses and local businesses. ASK!

If you fail to find any information about an organization from this, phone up the organization and speak to the receptionist. Ask them if they have a moment to tell you what the organization does. Ask for any brochures to be sent to you or ask for the website address where you might find that information.

The only exception to this rule is where you are applying to join the 'spy business' – especially government spy organizations. They are a bit of rule on to themselves…..

Going back to the rest of us, Brain Tracy (one of **America's** leading authorities on human potential and personal effectiveness) recounts the day that someone arrived at his office for a job interview:

"So, what do you do here?", he asked Brian.

Brian was flabbergasted – he has one of the most populated websites on the planet. He has written over 49 books, translated into 53 languages! Needless to say, the interview did not last long after that!

You need to find out as much as you can about any organization that you are going to spend any time in. This will help you determine whether they are a good fit for you as well as them working out if you will fit them. Further, when you know something about something, confidence builds. Energy builds. Motivation builds. These are all attractive to employers!

Play the Game: Research what your prospective employer does. What products and/or services do they provide? Who are their customers? Who are their competitors? Who are their suppliers? What issues are facing this particular sector at the moment? What issues might affect them in the future?

Reason #2

No energy.

When you talk with someone who has no energy, you are often left drained of energy. Try to think of when this has happened to you.

Now think of a time when someone was full of enthusiasm for something. What is the difference?

OK – if you really can't think of any situations, undertake a field experiment. If you have some youngish children (or some friends do) try the following:

Find out what they really are indifferent to (e.g. some water to drink works in my house). Offer them a drink of water – watch their faces and body language. Energy levels low? If not, you may have selected something the hate with passion – look for indifference!

Now offer them something that you know they really love (OK – chocolate in my house). Watch their face and body. What has happened? Yes – keen interest, alertness and most likely a smile of some sort.

If you present as an 'energy less' person at interview – you have very little chance of being offered a job. You will be seen as "just too much hard work to get moving". Remember energy is associated with moving, action and achieving. Most jobs require this. OK – the exception is being paid for sleep study research – where you are a 'sleeper'.

It is worth commenting here that this is not about being more vocal at interview. Many people make this error in assuming that lots of talk equates to energy. Quiet people can and do exude energy – indeed some of the best workers I know are people who do more and talk less! The trick here is to ensure you talk explicitly about the advantages of being "quiet" – it allows you to show you understand that at the end of the day it is what you are doing (taking action on) that adds value to the organization. If someone is talking all day about what they are going to do, but actually never get around to doing it – are they truly adding value to the business?

At any rate, this is a great subject to discuss at any interview. Why? Because it shows that you are thinking about things – and every employer prefers to have someone who thinks!

Play the Game: Find something that when you think about it makes you first smile and then floods you with some enthusiasm. This is your natural source of 'energy'. Before the interview, picture this energy giver in your mind – allow yourself to feel energized.

In the interview, if you feel your energy lagging, take a quick moment to visualize your picture of what gives you energy.

For me, this can be my dog or a memory of how I felt when I had just completed my PhD Viva (interview) and knew I had not only passed – but had no corrections to make. Wow-wee!

Now – find your picture or feeling to remember and use this simple technique to YOUR advantage.

Play the Game: The food you eat and the exercise you take affect your energy levels significantly. If you find that you often have low energy levels – you need to explore how your diet and exercise is influencing this situation. There are some simple quick aspects you can address – such as the eating of sugar (produces an insulin high followed by a 'drop off the cliff') through to eating high carbohydrate lunches, e.g. sandwiches – which usually guarantee a sleepy afternoon! However, it is not possible to do this subject sufficient attention here - this is a topic for another book!

Reason #3

Don't listen.

Many people think that interviews are about sending lots and lots of information AT the interviewers. They talk and talk and talk

When they do finally allow the interviewers to start asking a question, they rush in to finish their sentences for them – after all, they know what the interviewer is going to ask.

I'm afraid that these are classic signals of someone who is a poor listener. While nerves can contribute to the desire to talk and talk and talk – filling all silences with words, there is a good chance that you do this in your day-to-day living as well.

Poor listening skills is probably one of the most rapidly growing barriers to gaining a job, doing a job effectively and efficiently and of course to being promoted within an organization!

Most people talk themselves out of a job rather than into a job!

Play the Game: Practice listening to various people – really listening. When they stop talking, start your dialogue with "May I just check that I understand what you are saying.." Then summarize what they were saying. This forces you to listen.

It also enables clarity to be established – which is very important when people use a lot of subjective words – such as 'good'. For example, "How would you recognize good work versus poor work?"

Play the Game: Allow silences – they are opportunities to think. Remember the interviewers need to think as well. Filling silences usually results in you 'digging a hole' for yourself.

You know who you are if you are guilty of this. It really is up to you to develop healthier listening and speaking habits in all your life activities – work, home and social. They will thank you for it!!

Reason #4

Negative Mental Attitude

This is fairly easy for an interviewer to spot. It usually manifests itself when a candidate starts blaming something or someone for something that didn't quite go to plan.

One of the simplest questions interviewers can ask is "Tell us about a particular challenge you had at work/home/socially and how you dealt with it."

At this point, those with a negative mental attitude usually hurtle down the 'blame route'. This is particularly noticeable in management level interviews – where often 'everyone is to blame but me' is the message being given! Do this and it is usually the end of the road for your interview – expect them to finish up quite quickly.

So what are the interviewers looking for?

Yes – some sort of challenge you faced.

Yes – the dilemmas you may have had in deciding what to do (showing appreciation of the people and things involved in the issue).

Yes – how you took your positive mental attitude to solve or improve the situation. E.g. asking 'what could we do to improve the situation?' and holding a quick team brainstorm to gain options.

Yes – how positive mental attitude informs the decision making process.

Yes – that, even if the actions taken didn't quite work as initially planned, that your positive mental attitude enabled you to learn from the 'failure'.

Remember that people who aren't learning are going backwards – every situation, but especially situations where things don't go quite according to plan are YOUR opportunities to learn – if you allow yourself! More about this at **Reason #13: Confuse Years Worked with Experience**.

Play the Game: Practice positive mental attitude. Never blame anyone or anything during an interview. Demonstrate that you know how to problem solve on your own and through others. Demonstrate that EVERY situation is an opportunity to learn – including the interview you are in!

Reason #5

Discuss previous employers inappropriately.

Sadly this is another common 'game ender' at an interview.

It usually happens in response to the question "Why do you want to leave your current organization?"

I'm afraid that if you say anything bad about your employer (as an organization) or as an individual (your manager for example), those interviewers immediately jump to the thought that you will 'bad mouth' them when you come to move on from their organization. This makes YOU an unattractive option!

I know some of you will be sitting there saying "But my organization is truly awful." Or "My manager thinks I am a slacker because I am only in the office 12 hours a day and then tells me that I need to work harder."

These are very valid reasons for seeking to leave a particular organization. However, your interviewers are likely to know if your organization has the reputation of being a poor employer. They really don't want to know about your manager – they want to know about YOU.

Therefore, you need to turn this around into the positive – and discuss your ambitions. Discuss your wants, needs, dreams, goals, objectives.

A reasoned argument might run something like "I am excellent at delivering on goals such as X, Y and Z. I now want to continue growing my skills and level of performance, so I am looking for a role that will enable this."

Notice – you are implying that there is no such opportunity at your own company at the moment. They may ask you directly about this – and you may want to prepare a response that there is little opportunity for growth there at the moment – while that may change in the future, you are keen to make progress in a more deliberate fashion.

No matter how much they try to "pump" you for information about your employer or previous employers – simply respond with a "I don't think it would be appropriate for me to comment on that."

Another way to think about it is, when you join any organization, imagine you are signing the (in the UK) the Official Secrets Act – this means you don't talk about your employers or organization outside of work. Actually, this is quite a good approach to take generally and all the time – especially when you meet friends for a drink.

Play the Game: You can prepare your responses carefully BEFORE an interview. Make it about YOU, not your employer.

Play the Game: Show your integrity and loyalty by refusing to discuss organizational details which are outside of the public domain. If the interviewers become 'crusty' with you, I would suspect that you have been invited to an interview for them to find out something about your organization. This does happen – it has happened to me on several occasions… and no I didn't get the jobs. Indeed, I didn't want to work for them after the interviews!

Reason #6

Basing your Discussions on Opinion.

Everyone has opinions – it doesn't make them "right" and it doesn't make them "wrong".

Notice when an interviewer gives you an opinion – sometimes these are deliberately provocative in order for them to see how you react and manage people. This is an opportunity to show that you can have empathy with people's views, but you don't necessarily share those views or agree with them.

Good ideas (and words) to use here include "Everyone has their own perspective on a situation"; "gaining clarification of how everyone sees something can be very useful in generating ideas – as we all tend to see things slightly differently"; "that could be one opinion, I might look to see what supporting evidence there is for that opinion or for other possible views."

Play the Game: For every statement/point you make, think about what supporting evidence you could provide.

Play the Game: Practice these types of discussions with your family and friends – do explain beforehand what you are trying to achieve, so that they don't take offence at you challenging their opinions!

Play the Game: At interview, try to notice when you are being provided with an opinion – remember it is usually not about providing the 'right' answer to that opinion – but rather how you handle the situation of discussing opinion. You never know, you might evaluate the given opinion using some evidence and agree with the interviewer!

Play the Game: Acknowledge that a response you have given is indeed 'opinion' based – clarify that in the ideal world you would want to verify it with some evidence.

For example, someone might be of the opinion that a cluttered desk indicates a cluttered mind. The interviewer might ask you what you think about that and how does that relate to your own desk. I might respond with the discussion point "Well if a cluttered desk indicates a cluttered mind, I wonder what an empty desk indicates?"

Then I might go on to discuss using evidence based reflections about my own working style – Liking to have space to set out books, papers, 2 computers, timers and lights – but then putting away the materials at the end of the day to ensure I switch off my thinking on those subjects – allowing my brain to rest and regenerate.

OK – this hits a number of those devious little questions interviewers like to explore – such as working extra hours, personal organization, work-life balance and expectations about the working environment.

Reason #7

Being a Know-it-all.

Actually 'Know-it-alls' quite often do really well at interview – they usually manage to impress. Of course at interview you will always be dealing with people who are further up the food chain and usually know most of it as well. Interviewers may or may not view the 'know-it-all' as arrogant – much depends on the situation.

Depending on the 'smarts' of the interviewers, they may take the approach of a "How do you ensure you keep up to date?" type question.

The challenge comes when you go to meet the team – colleagues in different sections of the organization. This is usually part of the interview process – and these people's opinions will be asked for and taken note of.

I have seen so many people launch out of the main interview, where they were clearly on 'best behavior', only to act as a complete arrogant 'g-t' (you work it out) when they meet people in the organization. They of course, score zero points from the team!

A team that says 'no way' is very powerful when it comes to job offers!

Play the Game: No one knows everything. Be comfortable in acknowledging that you do make an effort to keep up to date – but what you don't know, you know how to find out. Hey – it is the information age – and there is so much online!

Play the Game: Be knowledgeable but respectful when you meet any employees in the organization. Be more interested in them and the organization than in showing off!

Reason #8

No Passion – for role, company/organization, customer, product, service.

This is different from **Reason #2 that of No Energy.**

Someone can have lots of energy – just not for the role, product, service, organization that they are currently working for or applying to.

A recent Gallup survey found that 71 per cent of American workers were 'not engaged' or 'actively engaged'. Similar levels of disengagement at work have been observed across a number of UK sectors. What does this say about their passions?

So most of these people have energy – for holidays, weekends, bowling, meals, games. However, they have no passion for their working life.

So if you can develop passion for something, do you think this might put you above all those applicants who lack passion? I think so.

So look carefully at the role, organization, customers, products, service and find something that you can get excited about – you only need one thing to start with.

For example, say you are a sales person. Become passionate about the number of "no"s you get. Why is this a great area to become passionate about? If you convert 10% of your calls into prospects, the more calls you make, the more prospects you develop. It's a numbers game. The more times you hear "no", the more times you will hear "yes".

This is not rocket science – and yet many sales teams sit dreading the point that they have to start making calls. Turn it into a game and enjoy – breathe passion into your attitude. You may find that it becomes contagious and other parts of the role become more interesting and offer up the opportunity to become passionate about.

Play the Game: Show some passion for at least one part of the role, organization, service or product. Always show passion for the customer – remember they pay you! Without that spark of passion, you will be seen as one of the statistics – an employee who has an 71% chance of hating their job.

Reason #9

Unable to demonstrate ability to manage self (and time).

Virtually every interview will ask you something about how you manage yourself – and in particular your time.

Interviewers are looking for someone who is busy for the right reasons. What are those 'right reasons'?

A. Doing as a high a value job as they can – so this means attending to those activities which add the most to the organisation.

This clearly will be different for every role – and it is worth asking the interview panel what they consider to be the most important tasks given in the job description (which of course you have; have studied; and brought with you to the interview – just in case you forget the key tasks.)

However, the interview panel can often ask you what you think are the most important tasks – and usually you want to look at the section which has a heading of "Key" or "Main" responsibilities or duties.

For many jobs this means that many tasks, often easy tasks, don't add much value to the organization.

Examples of these can be checking emails (unless this is your role of course), responding to texts, checking social media, opening mail, filing stuff away. These are tasks to be restricted to the 30 minutes before lunch and the 30 minutes before going home.

Your prime time needs to be focused on delivering your high value tasks.

Play the Game: If you haven't read **"Eat that Frog" by Brain Tracy** – go read it. This will help you understand and implement better management of your own work. Further, it will provide you with a methodology to discuss at interview – it is easy to explain and often attracts the attention of the interview panel due to its strange title!

B. Managing the quality of your work.

Recognizing when you are tired and liable to make mistakes is an important part of knowing yourself.

Once upon a time I used to work as a programmer. I had great focus in the mornings and could make excellent progress (about 3 times the pace of my fellow programmers). However, from about 3.00 pm onwards, my eyes would be tired and my brain became sluggish (at least sluggish for me). Therefore, between 3.00 pm and home time I would do other (less valuable) tasks. My manager once came in and shouted at me (it was about 3.30 pm and he was a very young manager) that I was supposed to be programming. All the heads in the room sunk down towards their key boards. I turned to our manager and I said "Graham, programming now, I can make more mistakes in 15 minutes than I can fix in 3 days!" Graham scuttled back to his office with a "Hmmph!" and my team mates broke out into smiles!

This was less about Graham the manager and more about me knowing myself – and taking responsibility to both progress high value tasks at the right time and stop when my own physical abilities had deteriorated. This was 'self-management' in action.

Play the Game: Think about when the quality of your thinking and work is at its best. Allocate this time to your highest value tasks – and do them until they are complete or the quality of your work deteriorates to an unacceptable level.

C. Keeping Emotions in their right place

Interviewers like to explore how you manage your emotions and those of others.

Play the Game: If you don't know much about this read one of my books (available on Kindle from Amazon) on this subject:-

"Board the Success Train" by A. Diamond

This book will help you think about how you can manage and use emotion in decision making. Sharing it with colleagues is a useful way to influence a group. It is applicable to work, home and play.

D. Maintaining your Health

Employers want to know that you are looking after your own physical and mental health.

Expect to be asked about this.

Most candidates can answer something about physical health – with, yes I exercise; I eat sensibly; I drink lightly or not at all; I don't engage in drugs; I don't smoke.

Be warned some employers will test you for drug use!

Many employers will ask for a physical to be undertaken as a condition of any job offer.

The area that is often ignored by candidates until they are forced to discuss it, is mental health.

Regardless of your history, you need to have prepared what you will say and how you will discuss this issue. Remember, you will be playing as part of a team – and team players look after their colleagues. This includes managing stress, depression and other, often hidden, mental health issues.

Play the Game: Research a little about maintaining mental health before the interview – so that you are prepared to discuss this topic.

Reason #10

Don't play well with others.

Organizations are all about products and services. Or are they?

To deliver any product or service you need to be able to relate to others. The first group you need to relate to are the customers/consumers/users of the product or service your organization provides. The second group are all the people involved in providing these products and services.

The clue is in the word 'relate'. You need to develop and sustain relationships with many different types of people.

In interviews you will be asked directly or indirectly about your approach to relationships, relationship building and of course examples of where you have developed and sustained different types of relationships.

The question is "How well do you play with others?"

Some might interpret this as team working – and yes, this is one element of the equation.

However, often roles require you to interact and deal one to one – especially with a customer.

Before you (and quite a few of you will be trying to do this) excuse yourself from this task of interacting with a customer:- "I work in product development – it is marketing's job to talk to the customer!", please.......

STOP!

This rationale is a perfect way to also excuse you from new jobs, promotions or developing truly outstanding products (and services). I admit to having heard this rationale far too often in interviews – and it is usually a 'show stopper' for that candidate!

So what do you need to do? Firstly, re-examine your concept of customer. It is not just the end (paying) consumer or user of your product/service. You have internal customers – those whom you supply something to.

This might be a component, a diagram, a clean bathroom, a report, answering the phone, greeting people at the door, guiding a pupil/student etc. Basically, every touch point in your day identifies another customer for you as an individual.

So for every 'customer', whether they are internal or end users, you have some sort of relationship with them.

You need to show your interviewers that you proactively manage each and every relationship – they are all unique in nature. Further, they change over time.

Play the Game: Identify every touch point in your current workplace. If you are not working, identify every touchpoint in your life – friends, family, shop assistants, clubs etc. Identify them as a 'customer' to you. Work out how you foster and develop those relationships.

If you think you have no touchpoints in your life – find some!

Play the Game: This links strongly with **Reason # 3 Don't Listen.** Active listening is the key skill to help you determine how you can add value to your relationships.

Play the Game: "I only have suppliers!" This tends to indicate that you are a 'taker' in life. This is not playing well with others. Selfishness and arrogance are traits rarely sought by interviewers. However, they may be actively pursued by spy services! Link with **Reason # 7 Being a Know-it-all.**

P.S. You don't have to like the people you work with to be a good team player. So don't make this assumption – you can build good relations with people who share few of your values or interests!

Reason #11

No use of diagrams.

Most roles that you apply for offer the potential for you to show that you can do more than simply respond to questions.

Very often, there will be a whiteboard or flipchart in the room. This is usually there to see whether you can stand up and explain something at a flip chart or whiteboard – drawing up simple diagrams or bullet points.

Many people shy away from doing this. Only too often have I heard the excuse of "I can't draw" used to justify not even giving it a go! This is a real MISSED OPPORTUNITY.

I have invited people to draw up a quick diagram, maybe a mind map, maybe a flow diagram – to illustrate a point they are making. When they just sit there and look like the proverbial 'rabbit in the headlights' I know immediately that they are unlikely to be the candidate for my client.

This applies to most professions – from cleaners, to electricians to IT to managers – everyone can make a good impact with a simple diagram.

Further, you don't have to be a good artist (I am certainly not). Indeed, I relish the fact that my picture elements are so 'age 5' standard – I can usually raise a smile on most people's faces! However, the communication of the point is most definitely and deliberately at or above the level of the interview.

Play the Game: Develop around 4 different types of diagrams before the interview. Learn them.

At some point in the interview, make a point of clarifying something using a diagram. If they have a whiteboard or flip chart – ask if you can use that. Otherwise, take some paper with you and draw on that – turning it around every so often while you construct it to show and explain your thinking.

The 4 diagrams that I suggest are worth learning include

    a.   Mind map
    b.   Process flow
    c.   Hierarchy – turn it on its side and you have a decision tree!
    d.   Force field analysis (much easier than it sounds and useful in most situations)

If you don't know what these diagrams are or how to construct them – Google them.

P.S. When you write on a whiteboard with a flip chart pen, which of course does not rub off a whiteboard (and it does happen – sometimes deliberately to see how you react to the situation) – yes have your sigh of "Oh not again!" and smile. This might seem catastrophic – however, they will have a solvent spray to remove it.

If they don't have a solvent spray, suggest to them that if they get someone to write over all of your pen marks with a whiteboard pen, they then will be able to rub it off – OK with a bit of effort.

Always leave it for them to deal with unless they ask you specifically to clean it (not sure why they would do this unless you are applying for a job that looks after training and conference rooms).

Reason #12

Don't know, don't care how to look after co-workers

Hydration

Oxygen

Rest

Legal Rights

"ists" and "isms"

Flexibility

A 2012 joint-study from two London universities where researchers examined the grades and test results of 447 university psychology students, found that test-takers who brought a water bottle to the exam (only about a quarter of students overall) scored 5-percent higher than their classmates who didn't.

Further, the British Army work on the principle that a deficit of just 5% in hydration levels seriously affects the brain. They estimate a reduction in performance of 15-20%.

This is serious. It has serious implications in many work environments.

If you are running a team that is de-hydrated, their performance is always going to be less than expected and less than they are capable of. This leads to problems with motivation, energy and drive.

All because people become de-hydrated!

Play the Game: Drink water. Enable and encourage your staff and colleagues to keep hydrated.

Low Oxygen Levels is a most commonly overlooked as a contributing factor to poor meetings. When a group of people meet, they use up oxygen, they produce lots of carbon dioxide. You will notice that people become difficult, argumentative and tired.

Play the Game: Stop any meeting that is not going too well. Take a 10 minute break – send everyone out of the room; open up the window and door to let oxygen in. Turn on any air conditioning – not for the cooling or heat – but to improve the air quality. Resume your meeting – everyone will have re-oxygenated their blood through walking about somewhere (even they only went to the toilet). The meeting will be a lot easier to both run and make progress.

Play the Game: Notice aggravated or non-cooperative people – this often signals a lack of oxygen in a room (and possibly dehydration). It can happen in an interview as well – especially when several people have been interviewed in the room before you. If you think this is the situation, ask whether you can open a window or door, or put the air conditioning on. Explain the possibility that there is a deficit of oxygen if need be.

Rest – most of us have the occasional night out and it impacts on our sleep. However, most employment contracts do expect you to come to work in a reasonably well rested state.

So if you have someone who is working a second or even a third job and then comes to work for a "rest", action needs to be taken.

Play the Game: Ensure that you get adequate rest most nights. You have a responsibility to yourself, your colleagues and your employer. This is especially important if you work with hazardous materials or machines!

Legal Rights - If you are a manager, you do need to know something about people's legal rights. This is a question of taking an interest in this subject and ensuring you go find out about basic human rights as relevant to your country.

Play the Game: Research and know basic human rights as relevant to your work environment. This includes 'isms' and 'ists'. For example, ageism, racism, sexist, etc.

Flexibility – there are various needs for flexibility. Especially where an employee is caring for someone – such as a child, a disabled person, a parent.

You need to think through what flexibility is appropriate in your sector of work. For example, when a surgeon is operating, it could be difficult to be flexible if their child needs picking up from school. A patient's life is dependent on that surgeon completing the operation.

However, many jobs have the capability to offer some flexibility. This might include doing some work from home; arriving a bit later than normal or leaving a bit earlier than normal.

Of course, there is a difference between a temporary situation and a long lived situation. In the latter, it is better to seek and agree a method of working which will satisfy both parties rather than build resentment that the employee appears to be taking advantage.

Play the Game: Before any interview, think about how flexibility is increasingly needed in the workplace. Think about how it affects anyone you know – so that you have an example to discuss. You might want to consider an example where things worked out fine for both parties and an example which ended in tears. Think about how those tears could have been avoided.

You need to be able to think through these situations regardless of what level of employment you are applying for!

Reason #13

Confuse years worked with experience.

Some people have worked at a job for 10 or 20 years and proudly say that they have 10 or 20 years of experience. But do they?

Many people learn their job in about one year. After that they are repeating that job. This situation is the 'have ONE year's experience repeated 10 or 20 times.'

It is therefore critical that you demonstrate that you have progressed while you have been in a job – that you have continued to improve the value you add over the period of time you have been in that position.

Key areas to work on are thinking, continuous improvement, use of technology etc.

The great thing here is that if you have only a short employment history – you can pack it full of valuable experience. This allows you to compete with those who have been doing the 'same thing' for years!

Similarly, if you have lots of years of experience, you will need to show that you have progressed over those years – rather than just stood still (or even worse, gone backwards in comparison to change).

Play the Game: Before the interview, list out all the experiences (not years) you have had at work (paid and unpaid). For example, someone shouted at you. How did you respond? How should you have responded? How would you respond today? This demonstrates that you are leaning from your experiences and that this will benefit a new employer.

Play the Game: If you are relying on X years of experience to count for something, you must be able to demonstrate that you are at least up to date with techniques in your field.

Read. Research. Observe. YouTube it. Google it.

Reason #14

Don't accept responsibility

This is particularly popular in public sector candidates. In the public sector, often there are cultural norms which help you avoid taking full responsibility for your work. The chances are that if you are a public sector employee, you probably don't even recognize that this is happening or has happened to you.

However, cultural norms, such as signing a note or report with your job title rather than your name does not encourage personal responsibility. This is especially relevant where you are moved between posts every 2 or 3 years.

An audit of a public sector organization revealed 17 ongoing projects. None of which had a named project manager. Only one (rather junior technical manager) stood up to admit that he "probably had in role in managing one of the projects". This is one of the key reasons why public sector projects have over spent hugely in the past – by the time a project is 3 years old, there is no traceable responsibility!

This can make it very challenging for a public sector employee to gain employment in the private sector. If this is you, you will need to demonstrate personal responsibility before gaining employment in the private sector.

However, just because you are currently working in the private sector, do not assume that you are able to demonstrate responsibility. It takes confidence to own up to an error if you are working in a 'blame culture'. Where the punishment for any error is being shouted at, demeaned or even being fired, you have a blame culture. People learn to keep their heads down – in fear of being 'shot at'.

Personally, I don't want to work in such an environment – and if I found myself in such an environment would be keen to ensure that any future employer had a positive view on taking responsibility – for both errors and wins.

While I would NOT state explicitly that my previous employer had this poor blame culture, most intelligent interviewers will 'read between the lines' when you probe about the culture of a prospective organization.

Play the Game: Take responsibility for yourself at all times in everything. Be proud of this.

Play the Game: Know that you are not perfect (no one is). Therefore, you will (like everyone) make mistakes. The secret is to acknowledge that you have made a mistake and then be careful not to make another mistake on top of it. This is called concatenation of errors.

The easiest example of a concatenation of errors is to consider when you are driving your car. Something dashes out from the side in front of you. You have three basic choices:-

a. Brake
b. Hit it
c. Swerve

Let's say you decide to brake only. You slow up somewhat and then miss or hit the object. Chances are that you will sustain either no damage or some damage the object and your car.

Let's say you decide to hit the object – no breaking no swerving.

Likelihood that the object will be badly damaged along with parts of your car.

Let's say you decide only to swerve – but you swerve into oncoming traffic. You hit an oncoming car while travelling a full speed.

This is fairly catastrophic – two errors have been joined together here – swerving combined with no braking.

Of course you might swerve and brake – but you increase the chances of hitting something else – either oncoming traffic or a house or tree.

Now consider these scenarios where your attention to driving was poor – e.g. talking on the phone; driving while exhausted. Your reaction time is slowed down – which reduces breaking time.

Very quickly you start to concatenate errors which exacerbates any situation.

This, of course, is why you are encouraged to take breaks from driving and the use of phones is either illegal or restricted to hands-free.

Play the Game: This is not rocket science – develop some examples of where you think it is essential that you, as a member of society, needs to take full responsibility for yourself. This is a key ingredient for employers who hold values!

Reason #15

Make sure your focus is poor.

What contributes to poor focus? There are some 'easy' contributors to poor focus at interview. The classic culprits are dehydration, headache, too much caffeine, hangovers (yes I have interviewed a number of people who had hangovers!), sugar level drops due to eating sweets before the interview and of course eating inappropriate foods which don't quite sit in the system as well as they might. These are the obvious culprits.

The less obvious culprit is linked to how you use technology – particularly if you are already addicted or approaching addiction. How do you know if you are in this situation? Simple, lock your phone, iPad, computer and any other tech you have away for 4 hours during your 'awake' period – i.e. during your day.

Using a simple piece of paper and a pencil/pen, make a quick record every time you feel the urge to go check one of your devices. Build a tally (the 5 bar gate system works well for most).

Over a 4 hour period – how many times did you feel the urge to go check? Count your tally.

Now divide 240 by your tally. This gives you your average minutes of focus period.

For example, over 4 hours I glanced up for my phone 5 times; I thought about my emails 3 times; I thought about a Facebook post twice; I wanted to Google terms 4 times; I wanted to relax with a YouTube video 3 times.

This gives a total of 17 technology related thoughts or urges.

$240/17 = 14.12$ minutes – on average between these types of distractions.

And this is before I consider that during a 4 hour period I will have had other distractions such as going to the toilet, getting something to drink, someone interrupting me etc.

What this indicates is that cultivating a habit of focus is extremely challenging when we allow technology to become the driver for our life.

For example, one lady was posting to Pinterest over 200 times each day. When asked why – she explained that she need to record what was happening in her day and share it. She acknowledged that she was addicted. Imagine employing someone who would post personal items 200 times during a working day of 8 hours!

8 hours x 60 mins = 480 mins

$480/200 = 2.4$ minutes

Yes – this person could be posting something to social media every 2.4 minutes. How happy would you be to pay her to do some jobs in between posting every 2.4 minutes?

Do you notice how it is useful to look at a situation from the employers' point of view? It is easy to do this – simply think of the pay being given to someone as your own money. This will tell you fairly quickly whether the performance of someone is appropriate or not.

So let's look at what happens in interviews – if you have an addition to technology (be it mild), the chances are that you will struggle in any interview. The idea of turning off your phone (it is not enough to put it on silent – you will still feel it vibrating a message of some sort to you) will be stressful for you. This will come through in your interview.

Of course, you really could ensure that you do badly in the interview by leaving your phone on and answering it, texting or searching for something while in the interview. Yes – this does happen – often without any word of apology as well.

Your habits contribute to your focus. When you practice periods of focus on ONE thing, you develop the ability to focus. Sounds obvious? As you have seen from my calculations above, often your periods of focus are not as long as you might think them to be. In interviews, it is really easy to see when a candidate loses focus – you need to practice sustaining periods of focus.

Poor focus is often accompanied with poor listening skills. Therefore practicing listening to people will help you with your focus.

Play the Game: Start practicing at home – ask your partner, kids, or friends to tell you about their dream(s). This is a great way to practice listening skills, as dreams are often illogical, so you are less tempted to complete their sentences for them! This can help build you up to a full 5 minutes of focused listening! Maybe more – depending on the dreams!

Play the Game: Practice focusing on ONE activity for increasing periods. Work up to a period of 40 minutes without thinking of anything other than the task you are doing. This you can do well before any interview!

P.S. My teenagers just look at me with horror when I take their phones away from them – this will be a huge issue for them entering the workforce in the next few years. Generally, I expect this issue to climb the Top Twenty over the next few years! Remember, you will never practice focus when your phone is in the driving seat!

Reason #16

Demonstrate poor delegation capability.

This is often revealed during questions about time management.

One of the most common situations for someone to describe at interview is a challenge they had when meeting a deadline. This really is about discovering how you get on with people and delegate work to them.

Some of you may be sitting there thinking "But I don't have anyone reporting to me – so I can't delegate." WRONG!

Delegation is essential in all business. You may be the "bottom" of the ladder – but you can still delegate. You can delegate upwards sideways and at "angles".

What does delegating upwards look like? This means enrolling the skills of someone further up the organization to undertake tasks that are suited to them. For example, technical tasks that you are not competent to do; discussions with key customers; liaising with the media or politicians. All you have to do is ask – and you will be surprised that when someone is identified as being the most qualified to do a particular task, how, usually they will help out.

What does delegating sideways look like? This is necessary when there is a target to be met and you need more people similar to you to be able to achieve the target. Key here is ensuring that the target (some might call it a goal, an order, or a piece of work) becomes a shared target of the group. This can sometimes be tricky in organizations where the culture resembles 'silos'. However, you need to always ask – eventually someone will help you (unless you are a very arrogant person who never helps anyone else – in which case, you are probably on your own!)

What does delegating at 'angles' look like? This is where you bring in expertise and resource from outside of the organization. This might be technical expert, an accountant, legal expertise, political expertise, project management skills, plumber, electrician, painter, and plasterer – any requirement that cannot be met from inside the organization.

All of these approaches show that you can achieve something through others. It may be that you have not had to do this yet – but I bet you have been asked to help someone else – use that experience to show that you can 'play well with others' and know the importance of delegation.

At interview, many people provide poor examples of delegation. They often continue 'digging a big hole' when they state that they have far too much work to do….something.

Consider the story of Alex who came to a time management workshop identifying that the biggest issue for her was 'too much work'. This resulted in not enough time for proper planning, team development or much personal progression. She was also starting to feel stressed at work.

Analyzing her situation, Alex identified that she didn't always delegate effectively. She knew this because her team always went home on time and often weren't fully occupied during the working day. Whereas she worked to past 8.00 pm every night to try to complete her workload. She felt unable to take holidays!

Indeed a telling statement from Alex was "I know that I keep back work from my team – but that is because I can do it so much better than them."

This of course demonstrates poor delegation skills – that is easy to spot. However, it also demonstrates a vicious circle where Alex was not enabling her staff to improve. She was not coaching them to undertake tasks at a satisfactory level. This meant that she was doing their jobs plus her own job. No wonder she came to a course on time management!

Play the Game: Spot those questions about time management. They are a great opportunity to show your approach and skills in delegation, planning, coaching, team working and of course, managing your own time.

Reason #17

Unable to demonstrate competence.

The usual way to demonstrate competence in something is to take an exam in it.

This is great if exams exist that actually examine a particular skill. However, most exams tend to examine your ability to prepare for and undertake an exam!

Therefore, it is still essential you ensure that you do undertake (and pass) relevant exams. This is especially relevant where many people have the same qualifications. You do not want to be in the situation where you are not getting job offers because you don't have something fundamental like English and Math (assuming you are applying to an English speaking organization).

However, this is not the whole story. While at interview, you will need to demonstrate that you have some relevant competencies.

So what might a relevant competency be? These you can usually find in the job description/requirements.

You can easily list out the basic requirements for any role and then methodically work through them determining how you can evidence them. So for example, many jobs require "Good computer skills".

The first difficulty here is the use of the word "good" – what exactly does this mean? It is a subjective word and is likely to mean something different to you than it means to me. Therefore, it is worth asking before the interview whether they have any criteria available which might help you understand what they mean by "good.".

Sometimes, employers will send this out as a matter of course. Others will keep the criteria a "guarded secret" to be used in the interview.

If the situation is the latter, you will have to establish what you consider to a 'good' level of computer skills – so that you can discuss your skills in relation to the job you are being interviewed for.

For example, if the job includes recording and publishing short training videos to an organizational intranet, it would certainly be beneficial to have some knowledge, experience and skills with software packages such as Camtasia.

While WORD skills would also be useful – they may be considered as simply a 'given'. This role will expect some editing skills of video and sound. You could quite easily take along an example short video you have put together (e.g. I shot an underwater scene of my fish and then added soundtrack and commentary to it).

Play the Game: Be proud of what you have done – take some examples with you. In this example, have some of your work loaded up onto YouTube ready for you to show at the interview.

Play the Game: Work out what competencies they are likely to be interested in and then work out how you could demonstrate this actively during an interview. Take an example, report, photo, drawing, diagram, worked piece, blog piece, testimonial etc.

Reason #18

Don't understand or use the concept of the "Winning Edge"

Many people place huge expectations on themselves when they go into an interview. As a result, they often show excessive signs of stress. They think that to win at interview they need to be at least twice as good as the other candidates.

Understanding the concept of the "winning edge" can make a huge difference to how you both see interviews and subsequently perform in them.

How does the winning edge concept work?

Think of a horse race. There is a winner and then there is second place. Often the winner wins by quite a short distance – maybe 'just a nose'. The winning horse wins about 10 times more than the horse in second place. Does this make the winner ten times faster than the horse that came in second?

No! The winning horse is faster by just a nose.

Often in interviews, it is a very similar situation – there are 2 or more candidates who are very similar (over a range of criteria). How is a decision made then about who to offer the job to?

It usually comes down to some small advantage one of the candidates had over the others, i.e. they are just a nose ahead.

This is where asking for some specific feedback as to what criteria the winner was a 'nose ahead' on would be really useful to you. Why? Because then you can work on that area, so that you become a nose ahead of future fellow candidates.

Of course, you may argue, that different employers are looking for different things – and yes, this is true. However, as you work on one area at a time after each interview experience, you gradually improve your overall performance at interview.

Consider the situation where there are 10 key areas that might be evaluated at an interview. Rate your performance in each area as 1.0 – do this today.

Overall performance today =

1.0 x 1.0 x 1.0 x 1.0 x 1.0 x 1.0 x 1.0 x 1.0 x 1.0 x 1.0 = 1.0

Note that these key performance areas can be inter-related. For example, improving listening skills always improves thinking, reflection, confidence, understanding etc. This makes the numbers below the "worst case". Whereas, in reality, because some areas are inter-related, improvement will be more than shown here!

Decide on one area to improve by just 1% over the next 30 days.

Day 30 Overall performance =

1.01 x 1.0 x 1.0 x 1.0 x 1.0 x 1.0 x 1.0 x 1.0 x 1.0 x 1.0 = 1.01

You attend an interview and they suggest a different area where you need to improve – work on that for the next 30 days – improve it by just 1% (this is NOT a big ask is it?)

Day 60 Overall performance =

1.01 x 1.01 x 1.0 x 1.0 x 1.0 x 1.0 x 1.0 x 1.0 x 1.0 x 1.0 = 1.0201

You attend another interview and they suggest a different area where you need to improve – work on that for the next 30 days – improve it by just 1% (again, this is NOT a big ask is it?)

Day 90 Overall performance =

$1.01 \times 1.01 \times 1.01 \times 1.0 \times 1.0 \times 1.0 \times 1.0 \times 1.0 \times 1.0 \times 1.0 = 1.03031$

Each time you attend an interview – decide to work on one key area for the following 30 days.

Within 10 months you will be in the following situation – assuming you improve performance by just 1% over each 30 days.

$1.01 \times 1.01 \times 1.01 \times 1.01 \times 1.01 \times 1.01 \times 1.01 \times 1.01 \times 1.01 \times 1.01 = 1.1046$

i.e. you will have improved your overall performance by more than 10% - actually 10.46% by just improving one area by 1% at a time over a month. This is of course the effect of compounding – you gain more than a simple improvement.

Now consider how many of these areas are inter-related. This will add significantly to your overall performance.

THIS is how you develop your winning edge!

Notice that you only have to be a little bit better. Further, by setting small incremental improvements, your brain doesn't stress out at the changes you are making.

OK – I know that some of you will be thinking "I don't have 10 months to get a job – I need it now!" And it may be that you do need to source a job that brings you in some money rather than no money – but that may be a lower paid interim position while you work on the roles you really want to do for the next few years.

Play the Game: It is a game – ask them what you need to do to improve your interview performance by just a tiny amount. This you can do at the end of the interview – and because you are asking about a tiny amount, they will probably give you some useful ideas. Write them down while in the interview – to review later.

Play the Game: Then work on a single aspect of your performance solidly for the next 30 days. It must be at least 30 days. It should only be one aspect – otherwise you don't really start to master that element of your performance.

Reason #19

Have nothing to showcase your skills at the end of the interview.

Take a report to show them.

Take a piece of work you have done.

Take a photo of something you have done.

Take a testimonial from someone you have helped (could be a customer, colleague or in a voluntary context).

Take anything you are proud of!

Make sure you remove any sensitive material or names.

Have a list of questions – even if they have answered all the questions you prepared, go through them with a pencil, ticking them off (so that they see you are both prepared and meticulous). You will always have the final question to ask – that being about what small thing could you do to improve your performance at interview.

Key here – is that you MUST ask something at the end to leave them with a good impression of you. No questions = unprepared, lacking in thought, uninterested in our organization.

People remember the start and ending of something easier than the middle – make sure you end strongly!

Play the Game: Make sure you prepare a list of questions on a neat piece of paper.

Play the Game: Construct an example report (remove all references to any people or organizations – I just replace them with XXXX instead of names. Make it look great (get someone to help you with this if necessary – everyone needs a proof reader) – it is something that they will glance through rather than read in any detail – so it is all about impressions of what you can do. Do NOT leave the report with them! (You need it for an interview the next day...!)

Reason #20

Don't turn up, arrive late or wear 'different clothing' to the vast majority of the employees.

Any of these can scupper your chances.

Many organizations simply won't interview you if you are late. Under exceptional circumstances, they might re-arrange (I got stuck in a snow storm on my way to the venue – the organization understood and rescheduled.)

Clothes and hair can be a sensitive and opinion dominated discussion.

For over a year when I was doing my PhD, I shared an office with a lady called Louise – she had long blue, pink and green hair. One day I went into the ladies toilets and there was a stranger standing there. Then I looked again – it was Louise. She had brown hair and was wearing smart clothes.

Yes – I was absolutely astonished – and asked her what was going on. She had just been to Oxford University for an interview. "I know they will not give me the job if I do not appear more conventional – they will judge me on my clothes and hair, rather than on my thinking abilities."

Now Louise was one bright lady.

The next day – she was back to colored hair. Two weeks later she received an offer from Oxford. Two months later she started working at Oxford University – with her tri-colored hair!

When you 'make it', then you can wear what you want – until then, err on the side of conventional. Dress in clean, well-cared for clothes – as smart as you can afford. If in doubt, go stand outside the organization as employees go into or out of the building and notice what they are wearing – this will help guide you.

Sadly, some interviewers make decisions on some very petty dress issues. I once sat on an interview panel where the chairman examined everyone's shoes in the first few moments. From this he made up his mind whether to listen to the person or not!

Play the Game: Know where you are going to be interviewed. Dry run a visit to there – knowing how the traffic at that time of day works for your mode of transport. To have a chance of succeeding at an interview you must first TURN UP. Then turn up ON TIME.

Play the Game: Assume that you need to be clean and well presented. Err on the side of conservatism – at least until you get the job!

Final Thoughts

Now it is up to you to take action – to lean to play the game. Use the suggestions in this book and you will quickly improve your performance at interview.

Remember that each interview is not a "fail" – it is an opportunity to improve your performance.

Interviewees who know and follow these "rules of the game" tend to find roles that they are both good at and suit them in terms of their own values.

Remember, an interview works both ways – you will spend a lot of time with your new work colleagues, so you want to make sure they are up to YOUR standards.

About the Author

A.J. Diamond developed the "Top Twenty Reasons Why" series following repeated questions about how to make real progress quickly.

Advising clients and sitting in on a wide variety of over 300 interview boards, A.J. has constructed this insight to the reasons why people fail at job interviews.

In addition, using the negative brainstorm technique to collect data from wide-ranging sources has enabled the development of these succinct "quick win" books.

Forthcoming titles in the "Top Twenty Reasons Why" series are

Top Twenty Reasons Why: People Fail **Exams**.

Top Twenty Reasons Why: You aren't being **Promoted**.

Top Twenty Reasons Why: You aren't getting a **Pay Raise**.

Top Twenty Reasons Why: You have **Less Money** than others in the **Bank.**

Top Twenty Reasons Why: People **Divorce** in 2015

www.ingramcontent.com/pod-product-compliance
Lightning Source LLC
Chambersburg PA
CBHW070935180526
45168CB00003B/1084